When Goodbye Means Forever

Andrew Zosangzuala

Published by Golden Leaf Haven Publishing, 2023.

Table of Contents

Preface

In the echoes of farewell, we find the whispers of our deepest emotions, the shadows of our most profound experiences, and the lingering memories that refuse to fade. 'When Goodbye Means Forever' is a poignant and powerful collection of poems that delves into the complexities of love, loss, and the bittersweet beauty of memories that linger long after goodbye.

Within these pages, you will explore the fragile dance of human connection, the devastating beauty of irreparable loss, and the transformative power of love. Each poem is a tender reflection on the heart's capacity to love, to lose, and to remember, inviting the reader to embark on a journey through the shadows of goodbye.

Through the pages, you will witness the joy and the pain, the laughter and the tears, the moments of tender connection and the agony of separation. We see the beauty of love in all its forms, and the devastating consequences of its loss. We feel the weight of forever goodbyes, and the solace of memories that refuse to fade.

This collection is a testament to the enduring power of love, even in the face of irreparable loss. It is a reminder that goodbye is not always the end, but often a new beginning, a chance to rediscover ourselves, and to find meaning in the memories we hold dear.

May these poems be a solace to those who have loved and lost, a reminder that they are not alone in their grief, and that the heart continues to whisper its deepest truths even in the silence of goodbye. May they also be a celebration of the human spirit, which finds a way to heal, to hope, and to love again, even in the face of forever goodbyes.

Andrew Zosangzuala,
Aizawl
13th September, 2023

Tears Hang

Tears hang in limbo
Emotions too heavy to drop
Silent sorrow flows

Eyes glisten with pain
Yet the tears refuse to fall
Holding back the tide

A heart too full of grief
The dam breaks, tears finally fall
Cleansing the ache within

Tears Fall

Tears fall from tired eyes
Echoing through empty rooms
Cries in vain unheard

Desperate pleas pierce
Heartache lingers in shadows
Hope fades with each tear

Silent sobs echo
Lost in the void of sorrow
Aching for solace

Her Voice

Her voice resides deep
Within my heart, echoes sweet
A symphony complete

Melodic whispers
Carrying me away, lost
In her soothing tones

In the stillness, calm
Her voice touches my very soul
A guiding light, whole

Heart Bursts

Heart bursts into flames
Passion ignites deep within
Love burns bright and strong

Embers flicker, dance
Fiery pulse of desire
Inflamed hearts unite

Blaze of love consumes
Heart ablaze with burning fire
Searing heat of passion

Fading Memories

Fading Memories
A whisper of what once was
Haunting, yet tender

Tears mingle with smiles
A bittersweet symphony
Echoes of the past

Holding onto ghosts
Sweet sadness fills my heart now
Nostalgic sorrow

In Dreams

In dreams we wander
Lost in shadows, cold as stone
Dead to the world's touch

Eyes closed in slumber
Breath still, heart silent and still
In the realm of night

Ghosts of past linger
Haunting whispers in the dark
Dead to the world's light

Deep Breath

Taking a deep breath
I close my eyes and let go
Trusting in unknown

Heart pounding, I jump
Into the abyss of doubt
Faith guides my descent

A leap of faith taken
With open arms, I embrace
The journey ahead

Love Fades

Love fades like withered
Petals, dreams dissolve in tears
No happy ending

Promises shattered
Like fragile glass, hearts broken
No happy ever

Lonely hearts ache for
A love that will never bloom
No happy after

In Dreamland

In dreamland I walk
Through fields of fleeting memories
Lost in my own thoughts

Whispers of the past
Echo through my silent mind
A dance of shadows

In reverie I
Find solace in the stillness
A moment in time

Blood Trickles

Blood slowly trickles
Each cut brings closer to end
A thousand pains felt

Each slice a whisper
Silent screams of endless pain
A slow death awaits

Cuts deep, never ending
Life fades with each cruel cut made
Death by a thousand

In Silence

Tears fall in silence
Shattered love leaves empty space
Heartache lingers on

Fragments of a bond
Scattered pieces in the dark
Memories remain

Lonely hearts wander
Searching for the missing half
Hope flickers faintly

Cloaked In Lies

Mistakes cloaked in lies
Goodbyes mask the truth within
Farewell to deceit

Parting words conceal
Blunders swept away by tears
Concealing the past

Farewell to regret
Errors hidden in goodbyes
Mistakes left unsaid

Your Voice Fades

As your voice fades slow
Whispers linger in the air
Memories remain

Silence fills the room
Echoes of your laughter gone
Leaving me in void

Words once filled with life
Now drift away like a dream
Leaving emptiness

Cold Air Whisper

The cold air whisper
Wish you were here beside me
Underneath the stars

Lonely nights without
Your laughter and warmth to hold
Wish you were closer

Dreams of you linger
Heartache eases with each thought
Wish you were with me

Love's Grasp

In love's desperate grasp,
I'd do anything for you,
Even lose myself

Desire's fierce flame burns,
I'd do anything to quench,
In your sweet embrace

Boundless devotion,
I'd do anything, my love,
To prove my faith true

Can Wait Forever

Patiently I wait
Time means nothing in your arms
Forever with you

Every moment counts
Our love will endure and last
I can wait for you

Eternal promise
I will wait for you always
My heart belongs to you

Sharpen My Knife

I sharpen my knife
Tonight I plan to strike down
Tomorrow's sunrise

Whispers of my deed
Echo through silent shadows
Tomorrow's end nears

Darkness veils my path
Each step closer to my fate
Tomorrow's bloodshed

Dark Clouds

Dark clouds looming near
Whispers of despair run through
The beginning of the end

Shadows lengthen fast
Silent waves of change approach
The end is in sight

Fading light, a sigh
Final chapters unfold now
The end is upon us

Here Now

Without you here now
Silence fills the empty space
Your presence missed dear

I long for your touch
Echoes of your laughter fade
Lonely hearts do weep

Memories linger
Whispers of love in the air
Without you, I ache

Broken Pieces

Broken pieces lie
Scattered, lost in shadows deep
A puzzle incomplete

Fragments of my soul
Whispered echoes of my past
Fade into the night

Whispers in the wind
Memories of who I was
Falling into dust

Never There

In the dead of night
Your presence lingers, like mist
A haunting echo

Whispers in the wind
A ghostly apparition
Memories remain

Empty room, I wait
For the ghost of you to come
But you are never there

Desperate Pleas

Tears fall silently
Echoing in empty space
Sobs lost in the wind

Desperate pleas fade
Into the void, unheard, lost
A lone voice wails on

Heartache fills the air
Echoes of pain, cries in vain
Lonely sorrow's song

Silent Tears

Silent tears fall down
In the darkness of the night
Heartache lingers on

Shattered pieces lie
Scattered in the wake of love
Pain echoes within

Time heals all wounds, they say
But broken hearts still remain
Hoping for sunset

Hidden Mistakes

Mistakes hidden well,
Cloaked in bittersweet farewell,
Deception unveiled.

Parting ways in guise,
False goodbye to cover lies,
Truth waits behind eyes.

Farewell, a charade,
Disguising mistakes we made,
Truth will not evade.

Fragile Heartbeat

A fragile heartbeat
Struggles with every beat
Life hangs in the balance

Each step a gamble
Echoes of time running out
Fate's hand on his chest

His heart, a heavy burden
Weighted with fear and regret
His story near its end

Ashes Beneath

Ashes beneath my feet
Whispers of the past now gone
Standing tall, reborn

Embers fade to black
Yet I stand strong, unbroken
In the ashes I rise

Silent remnants sing
Of a fire once fierce and bright
Now I stand alone

Fading Dreams

Fading dreams whisper
The dawn breaks, reality
End of flight so sweet

Clouds drift, taking flight
Colors vanish, leaving grey
Dreams slip away softly

Morning light cascades
Gentle reminders of night
Dreams fade, now awake

Lost In Wind

Whispers lost in wind
Echoes of forgotten dreams
Haunting melodies

Silent breaths of love
Drift away like autumn leaves
Lost in solitude

Fading echoes fly
Lost whispers in the night sky
Searching for their home

Perfect

In perfect stillness
Nature whispers her secrets
In the tranquil night

A perfect sunset
Paints the sky with golden hues
Beauty in motion

Ah, perfection found
In the simple moments, where
Joy and peace collide

Sorrow

In shadows we weep
Tears silently falling down
Sorrow fills our hearts

Aching hearts, heavy
Grief consumes us day and night
Sorrow knows no end

Whispers of sorrow
Echo through the empty room
Only tears remain

There For You

In your darkest days
There for you, a guiding light
Bringing hope and peace

Friendship's sturdy bond
There for you through thick and thin
A love that endures

Loyal heart beats true
There for you through joy and pain
A constant presence

Mercy And Justice

In courts of law, truth
Balances the scales of justice
Mercy guides the way

To forgive, to heal
Acts of kindness and grace bloom
Justice served with love

In world filled with strife
Mercy softens hardened hearts
Justice finds its peace

Much Like Falling

Leaves gently drifting
Like whispers from the sky above
Nature's graceful dance

Autumn's embrace calls
Falling like the setting sun
A peaceful descent

Time slows as we fall
Embracing the unknown path
Finding beauty in descent

Chasm

A deep chasm yawns
Echoes bounce off rocky walls
Silence fills the void

Carved by ancient streams
Chasm divides earth's surface
Nature's fierce beauty

Adventurers leap
Across chasm's yawning gulf
Courage conquers fear

In The Dark

Shadows sway in night
Whispers of the unknown past
Lost in darkness' grip

Stars twinkle above
Guiding light in black abyss
Hope in darkest hour

Moon's soft glow reveals
Secrets hidden in the dark
Silent worlds collide

Swept Away

Caught in raging storm
Swept away by fierce currents
Lost in deep waters

Leaves dance in the wind
Swept away in graceful flow
Nature's gentle touch

Memories drift by
Swept away in time's embrace
Lost to the moment

Tiny Heart

Tiny heart pulsates,
Love flows through microscopic
Veins of tenderness.

Infinite feelings,
Contained within a small space,
Beating steadily.

Fragile and precious,
A tiny heart holds the world
In its gentle grip.

Bitter Sweet

Bitter sweet feelings
Tug at heart and soul deeply
A delicate dance

Joy and sorrow blend
In a tapestry of life
Each moment precious

Tears fall like raindrops
Cleansing the wounds of the past
Bitter sweet release

Violent Love

Scarlet passion burns
In tangled, fierce embrace
Love's pain leaves its mark

Bloodied hands that clutch
A heart that beats in rhythm
With a lover's rage

Whispers turn to screams
Passion's fire ignites the dark
Love's violence gleams

Light In Your Eyes

Sparkling, bright eyes shine
Like diamonds in the moonlight
Guiding me home safe

Sunrise in your gaze
Golden hues to start my day
Pure warmth in your light

Twinkling stars reside
Deep within your soulful eyes
A universe inside

Believe In Dreams

Believe in dreams bright,
They guide us through darkest night,
Hope takes to new height.

Whispers in the wind,
Dreams dance within our minds, find
Magic that's within.

Faith in dreams will soar,
Reaching for what's meant for more,
Believe and explore.

Bury Your Heart

Bury your heart deep
In soil, let roots intertwine
A garden of love

Deep in the earth's grasp
Protected from pain and hurt
Heart beats in silence

A secret treasure
Hidden, safe from the world's harm
Bury your heart deep

Saving Grace

Grace softly descends
Lifting burdens from our souls
A saving embrace

In darkest hours
Grace appears like a beacon
Guiding us back home

In times of despair
Grace whispers of hope and love
A light in the storm

Open Your Eyes

See the world around
Colors, shapes, and beauty lie
Open your eyes wide

Morning light streams in
Awakening the senses
Open your eyes now

Nature sings softly
Breathe in the magic of life
Open your eyes, dear

Burn It Down
Raging flames consume
The old, the broken, the lost
New life will arise

Inferno's bright glow
Purges all that once was known
Ashes drift away

Burn it down, start fresh
From the ashes, hope will rise
A phoenix reborn

In Loving Memory

Whispers on the wind
In memory, they linger
Love never fading

Gone but not forgotten
Memories etched in our hearts
Forever cherished

In loving memory
Hearts still ache, but souls find peace
A legacy lives

The End Is Here

The sunset arrives
Colors fade, day turns to night
End is near, goodbye

Leaves fall from the trees
Nature's cycle, time to rest
Seasons change, farewell

The final chapter
Closing, the end is now here
Embrace goodbye's touch

Before Tomorrow Comes

Before tomorrow
A fleeting moment in time
Live in the present

Whispers in the night
Promises of a new day
Hope on the horizon

Stars fade into dawn
Time marches ever forward
Embrace the unknown

Ghost Of Days Gone By

Whispers in the wind
Echoes of old memories
Ghost of days gone by

Fading photographs
Tales of laughter and sorrow
Haunting in their charm

Shadows of the past
Lingering in empty rooms
Ghosts of what once was

All Hope Is Gone

All hope is now lost
Darkness consumes every soul
Despair fills the air

Faded dreams lie still
Shattered promises remain
Hope's light fades away

A world devoid of
All traces of hope and light
Silent cries echo

Still Remains

Soft whispers in breeze,
Memories linger, unfazed,
Love's touch still remains.

Faded photos shine,
Laughter echoes through the years,
Joyful moments stay.

Silent nights recall,
Moonlight dances on the past,
History endures.

Life Must Go On

Life must go on now
Through every storm and struggle
We find strength to face

Sorrow and joy mix
In the rhythm of our days
Never stopping long

Time marches forward
Leaving us to move with it
Embracing the change

Addicted To Pain

Each cut a release,
A temporary solace.
Pain becomes addict.

Lost in the darkness,
Seeking solace in the pain.
Addiction takes hold.

Numbness fades away,
Pain becomes the new normal.
Addicted to hurt.

The Uninvited

Uninvited guest,
Intruding on sacred space,
Unwelcome presence.

Uninvited soul,
Lurking in shadows unseen,
Bringing discord near.

Uninvited storm,
Raging through tranquil waters,
Disrupting peace's calm.

Calm The Fire

Flames quiver and dance
Flickering in the darkness
Embers glow softly

Whispers of a breeze
Tames the raging inferno
Silence reigns supreme

Cool waters awaken
Quench the fiery intensity
Tranquility restored

All Ends Well

In the darkest night
Hope shines through with morning light
All ends well in sight

Clouds part, sun breaks through
Joy and peace fill the heart true
All ends well is due

Storms may rage and swell
But in the end, all is well
Love's light always dwells

The Last Hero

The last hero stands
Brave and resolute in fight
Hope rises within

Legends told of him
Courageous, selfless, noble
A savior at last

Darkness closing in
The last hero rises strong
Light shines from within

The Other Side

Cross the threshold now
Where darkness meets the unknown
A new world awaits

Mysteries unfold
Whispers of the other side
A realm unseen, felt

In shadowed stillness
Echoes of eternity
The other side calls

Poison In Your Veins

Venom courses through
My veins, toxic and deadly
Slowly consuming

Bitter taste of lies
Infected blood, tainted soul
Poisoned from within

Deadly thoughts invade
Sickened heart, damaged spirit
Poisoned by my own

Cradle To The Grave

From cradle to grave
Life's journey is but a blink
In time's endless stream

Infant cries softly
Elderly hands tremble close
Circle of life flows

Each breath a heartbeat
From birth to final sunset
Life's dance never ends

Walk The Sky

Stretching to the stars
Our feet barely leave the ground
Yet we walk the sky

Clouds beneath our feet
The world so far below us
As we wander high

Step by step we rise
A journey among the clouds
Walking in the sky

The Bitter End

Dark clouds overhead
The bitter end draws near now
Heartache fills the air

Petals falling fast
Lost in the winds of change now
Whispers of goodbye

Empty echoes ring
In the silence of the night
A bitter farewell

Dying Light

Darkness creeps closer
Eclipsing the fading light
Lingering twilight

Sun slips below the horizon
Colors blend and fade away
Night-time claims its throne

Whispers of farewell
The last rays say their goodbyes
Dying light surrenders

Further From Myself

Lost in the distance
Further from myself I roam
Seeking to be found

Echoes of my past
Drift further into the void
Lost in time's embrace

I follow the path
Away from where I began
Towards the unknown

When Tomorrow Comes

The sun will rise high
Bringing hope for a new day
Tomorrow blooms bright

Dreams wait in the dawn
Opportunity beckons
In each fresh sunrise

Tomorrow's promise
Carries endless possibilities
Embrace the unknown

I Fade Away

In shadows I'm lost
Memories slowly dissolve
Fading into night

Whispers of the past
Silent echoes in the wind
As I drift away

A fleeting moment
I disappear into mist
Leaving no trace behind

Forever Starts Now

Eternal cycle
Time everlasting and true
Forever begins

Infinite moments
Endless love and devotion
Forever unfolds

Forever's embrace
Boundless joy and endless peace
Now and always true

Fire On The Inside

Locked in a fierce blaze
Burning passion deep within
Yearning to break free

Embers smoldering
Heart aflame with desire
Aching to ignite

Flames dance in my soul
Radiating warmth and light
Eternal fire burns

Secrets And Regrets

Hidden in shadows
Whispers of past mistakes made
Regrets fills the air

Silent tears fall down
Secrets buried deep within
Weight of guilt consumes

Mistakes left unsaid
Haunting memories linger
Regrets never fade

Will You Be There

Will you be there, love
In the silence of the night
My heart longs for you

Whispers in the wind
Promise of a gentle touch
Will you be with me

Through the stormy seas
I search for your steady hand
Will you be my guide

Lost It All

In the dark of night
I search for what once was mine
But all is now lost

Memories fading
Like a distant dream now gone
I have lost it all

Empty is my heart
Aching for what I once had
Lost in the shadows

Shooting Star

A flash in the night
Shooting star across the sky
Wish upon its light

Momentary spark
Trailing beauty in its wake
Fleeting wish to make

Silent streak of gold
Falling through the darkened sky
Dreams follow its path

Ember Of Hope

With every flicker,
Embers of hope ignite bright,
Guiding us through dark.

In the coldest night,
A small ember of hope burns,
Giving warmth and light.

Hope's ember flickers,
Guiding us through life's storms dark,
A beacon of light.

Embrace The Chaos

Chaos entwines us
In its depths, we find peace
Embrace the swirling

Minds in disarray
Finding order in the storm
Chaos brings comfort

Embrace the chaos
In its madness, we find calm
Let go of control

Cold Hearted

Frozen embers burn
In a heart turned to ice
Love's flame extinguished

Icy glares pierce through
Nothing but chilling silence
No warmth to be found

Cold heart beats alone
Frigid walls keep love at bay
Emotion on ice forever

As She's Walking Away

Silhouetted grace
Whispers of her presence fade
Heartache in her wake

Footsteps growing faint
Memories of her linger
Fading into night

Gone with the twilight
Lost in the shadows, she fades
A fleeting goodbye

Keep Me In Mind

In your thoughts, please keep
me drifting on memory's breeze
fading with each day

In the quiet night
mind wanders to thoughts of you
hold on to me tight

Like petals in wind
I float through your mind, unseen
keep me in your thoughts

Goodbye In Her Eyes

Eyes filled with sorrow
Whispering silent goodbye
Tears betray the truth

Emotions hidden
Fleeting glance says it all
Love lost in her eyes

Aching hearts collide
Goodbye etched in every blink
Farewell in her eyes

Day That I Die

As I fade away
Sunset colors fill the sky
Embracing the end

Whispers of farewell
Leaves rustling in the wind
Life's final chapter

Memories linger
In the hearts of those I love
In death, I am free

Tomorrow Never Comes

Tomorrow never
comes, always just out of reach
live in the moment

Dreams of tomorrow
fade with the setting sun's light
grasp today's beauty

Chase not after time
for tomorrow is a myth
embrace the now, live

Between Heaven And Hell

Between heaven's light,
and hell's fiery lament,
lost souls wander on.

Caught in limbo's grasp,
struggling to find their way,
amidst eternal struggle.

In the realm between,
hope flickers like a candle,
guiding souls to peace.

Way Beyond Empty

A hollow echo
Way beyond empty now
Lost in the void's grasp

Silent stars above
Whispers of a distant past
Emptiness reigns here

Soul adrift in void
Echoes of lost dreams linger
Beyond empty now

Too Numb To Cry

Feeling so empty
tears won't come to my tired eyes
numbness fills my soul

Heartache grips my chest
but no tears fall from my eyes
numbed by sadness's hold

Emotions run deep
but my tears have all run dry
numbness clouds my mind

Lost Prayer

Lost prayer drifts in wind
searching for way to return
to its rightful home

Echoes through the night
silent pleas reach the heavens
lost prayer finds its way

Whispers in the dark
a lost prayer finally heard
answered with the dawn

Darkest Hour

In the darkest hour
stars twinkle in the black sky
guiding us through night

Shadows stretch and yawn
moonlight whispers secrets dark
night's embrace holds tight

Darkness envelops
but dawn always breaks through the
promise of new light

Eyes Of Burden

Heavy burdens weigh
upon weary eyes, cast down
in sorrow's shadow

Dark circles linger
haids of stress and sleepless nights
bearing heavy loads

Eyes reveal the strain
of burdens carried alone
seeking solace's light

Forgotten Memory

A faded picture
in the corners of my mind
lost to time's cruel grip

Whispers of laughter
echo through the empty halls
a memory fades

Forgotten moments
drift like leaves in autumn wind
lost in the silence

Yesterday's Tears

Memories once clear
now blurred by yesterday's tears
sorrow fades with time

Silent drops cascade down
yesterday's tears, a river
flowing back to me

Like rain on my face
yesterday's tears cleanse my soul
renewal begins

Useless Apologies

Empty words spoken,
Apologies lack meaning,
No change is made here.

Regrets are worthless,
Without actions to support,
Lip service won't do.

Apologies fall,
Like leaves in autumn's embrace,
Fading into air.

Living In Your Letters

Ink on paper swirls
Capturing moments in time
Words from the heart speak

Sent across oceans
Feelings of love and longing
In each stroke they dwell

Paper stained with tears
Memories etched in each line
Living in your words